The Resilient Advisory Business

Systems for Business Optimization & Growth

S. Jay Coulter, CFP®, CIMA®

© 2019 S. Jay Coulter

Table of Contents

Introduction

Financial advisors, teams and firms are under a lot of pressure today. If you've picked up this book, you know the sources of this pressure all too well: new regulations, fee compression, changing tech stacks, client portfolio performance and firm policies that lead to professional stress.

In my work with some of the industry's top performers over the last 20 years, I've learned optimal ways to implement business systems that free up time, drive growth and build a thriving practice. This book is designed to be a granular resource for advisors who want to build customized systems for their business.

This is the exact process that I take advisors through in my coaching and consulting program. These systems will help the reader transform their practice into a self-running business. I have seen these systems help advisors change the course of their careers.

There are few careers more important than that of a financial advisor. A professional, competent and empowered financial advisor will have a fundamental impact on the lives of the people they serve. My professional purpose at this stage of my career is to serve investors and the financial advisors who serve them.

In my first book focused on financial advisors, I taught readers about the **Protocol System**. This system helps advisors who are weighed down by stress. In my experience, there is a stress epidemic in our industry. If you find yourself overwhelmed by extreme stress, please grab a complimentary copy of **The Resilient Advisor** (jaycoulter.com/raebook) and take care of yourself before implementing the business systems detailed in this book.

The Three Success Drivers

If you have picked up a copy of this book, you are most likely interested in changing something about your advisory business. I have worked with financial advisors for over two decades, and in the pages that follow, I will outline the systems I have seen deliver the most effective results.

For the last several years, I have enjoyed producing **The Resilient Advisor Podcast** (jaycoulter.com/listen) as well as a YouTube channel (youtube.com/c/JayCoulter) focused on helping financial advisors improve their businesses and lives. This has given me the opportunity to interview thought leaders from the fintech, practice management, marketing and investment management space. I have learned their best practices and thoughts on what will shape the advisors of the future. These are exciting times to be a financial advisor!

Every author, consultant, coach and/or speaker has a model to frame their message. This makes it easier to sell books, keynote speeches, and trainings. My simple model was developed through research and real-world application working with financial advisors. I've had the opportunity to work with and model the best in the industry. Top performers are committed to excellence in three areas I call the "*Success Drivers.*"

These are:

FOCUS, SYSTEMS and RELATIONSHIPS

1.   **Focus** – In reality, the top performers have RADICAL FOCUS. In my consulting practice, one of the first items we address at the start of an engagement centers on the proper way to set and achieve goals. Personal and professional goals are critical to mapping out where you want to go, but very few financial advisors spend time on this

important exercise. We have a joke at my firm, but in reality, it is not funny. When we ask a new client where they want to be in five years, 90% of the time we get one of two responses:

1. I want to double my business.
2. I want to be a million-dollar producer.

They heard someone say achieving million-dollar producer status is a great goal or they arbitrarily decided they would like to make twice as much money. A successful advisor is laser focused on what is important. Everything else that is not critical to the success of the business is systematized or outsourced. They know the exact success drivers of their practice and that is where they spend their time. The system I use is a tool that dominates the Silicon Valley, but I have customized it for financial advisors. It is called OKRs, and you will learn about in this book.

2.   **Systems** – Building systems to accomplish the necessary tasks in running your practice and personal

life is mandatory. It is not possible to efficiently grow without business systems in the complicated industry we work in today. Also, once business systems are in place, most financial advisors find they have more free time in the day for business development. In this book, I will teach you how to build the **Four Core Business Systems** every advisor must have if they want to achieve success.

3.   **Relationships** – I have repeatedly told my young children, "At the end of your days, time and relationships are all that you will value." Personal relationships and business relationships are such an integral part of any success a financial advisor will have. One of the systems I will teach you in this book centers on building, nurturing and growing your relationships. Andrew Carnegie, the wealthiest man of

his generation, said, "No man becomes rich unless he enriches others."

In the following chapters, I will show you exactly how radical focus coupled with the right well-oiled systems will help you build a Resilient Advisory Business™.

The Systems

This book shows financial advisors how to build the **Four Core Business Systems** that enhance the "Success Drivers" for any advisor, team or firm. These pages were designed to drive action and lead you down a path to implement the systems that are discussed.

Once these four systems are implemented, you will have built a Resilient Advisory Business™:

1. OKR Goal Setting & Leadership System
2. Client Experience System
3. Wealth Management System
4. Relationship Marketing System

Let's get started!

Chapter 1: OKR Goal Setting & Leadership System

The first system we'll examine in this book is the power of identifying and measuring OKRs for financial advisors, teams and firms. This framework originated in Silicon Valley, and the acronym stands for **Objectives and Key Results**. It is a simple yet game-changing system for leveling up your business through leadership, accountability and goal setting.

The Beginnings of OKRs

In 1979, Intel was at a crossroads. Its flagship 800 microprocessor was coming under attack from startup competitors, but more importantly, from Motorola. Motorola had introduced their 1600 microprocessor, and not only were they taking market share, the Motorola product was a better performing microprocessor. Andy Grove was the president and COO of Intel at the time. He held an emergency retreat at the end of 1979 with his team to figure out what to do.

That retreat proved to be a turning point for the company. Out of it grew a new commitment to take on Intel's rivals and level up its product offerings. The company leveraged Grove's existing OKR system to build a plan to crush Motorola. That plan was famously named "Operation Crush" after the Denver Broncos' dominant defense of the late 1970s.

Silicon Valley Embraces the OKR System

One of the product managers at Intel during this time period was a gentleman named John Doerr. John ended up leaving Intel in the early-1980s and joining the Silicon Valley firm Kleiner Perkins. In 1999, he added Google as a portfolio client to its roster of highly visible tech companies. In his first meeting with Larry and Sergey, allegedly around a Ping Pong table, John outlined the concepts and constructs of an OKR system. He intelligently described how it had helped Intel manage its growth through the 1970s and crush Motorola in the 1980s.

After that first meeting, the Google leadership team saw the benefits of an OKR system and implemented one immediately. The results speak for themselves. Today, Google is one of the biggest companies using OKRs to drive growth. However, Google is certainly not the only company in Silicon Valley to leverage an OKR system to manage goal setting and accountability. Others include Dropbox, AirBnB, Spotify, Twitter, LinkedIn, Facebook and Amazon. OKR systems are not just limited to the tech space. BMW and Disney also use this powerful tool.

Nonprofits Benefit from OKRs

In 2000, Bill and Melinda Gates set up the Gates Foundation. Right from the beginning, it had a unique problem. On the one hand, it was a startup. On the other, it was instantly the largest nonprofit in the world. Patty Stonesifer was put in charge of running the foundation. She found herself quickly overwhelmed, but fortuitously, sitting in on a board meeting for Amazon, heard about the OKR system and how it was impacting the company in an impactful way.

Stonesifer asked John Doerr to come in and present the concept of the OKR system to the board of the new Bill and Melinda Gates Foundation. They implemented it, and the concept has driven fantastic results. In fact, Bill Gates says that when it came to scoping out funding opportunities, "The OKR System made me confident I was making the right call."

Bono, the lead singer of U2, is also one of the world's most notable philanthropists. His organization, the One Campaign, went through a change where they merged with another nonprofit so they could jointly attack some of their big, audacious goals. That merger created some cultural challenges inside the organization. Bono asked John Doeer to come in and present the OKR structure and concept to the nonprofit. It helped them drive results.

Bono says, "OKRs saved us, really. OKRs forced us to think clearly. They sharpened our strategy, our execution, and our results."

For a deep dive on OKRs and their impact on the Silicon Valley, I suggest John Doerr's fantastic book *Measure What Matters*.

 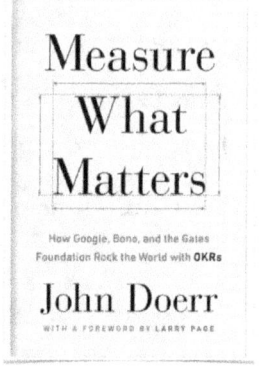

OKRs for Financial Advisors and Teams

Given the highly effective nature of OKRs on these successful companies and organizations, why have we not heard about them as financial advisors? OKRs are simple by design. They stand for Objectives and Key Results:

> An **Objective** *is an ambitious and aspirational goal that makes you a little uncomfortable.*

> **Key Results** *are clear and measurable results that will lead to achieving the objective.*

An example of OKRs: The most popular way to describe and understand how OKRs work in practice is by looking at an NFL franchise. The General Manager has one Objective: make money for the owner. Potential Key Results for a General Manager, then, could include winning the Super Bowl and having home game attendance exceed 98% capacity.

Achieving these two Key Results will generally make money for the owner of the NFL franchise.

To show you how this would then flow through the organization, the Head Coach and the Head of Marketing would have the own OKRs that flow directly from those of the General Manager. The Head Coach would have an Objective to win the Super Bowl. You can see how this clearly aligns with the General Manager's OKR, and more specifically, to his Key Results. The Head Coach knows that today, to win the Super Bowl, you need two Key Results:

1. To build a top five statistical defense.
2. To average 4.3 yards per carry.

In other words, the team needs a dominant defense and a great running game.

Now, the Head of Marketing will have a different set of OKRs. Speaking to the Key Results of the General Manager, the Head of Marketing's Objective is to maintain home game attendance above 98%. To achieve this Objective, the Marketing team could seek two specific Key Results:

1. Run four summer promotional campaigns to encourage new season ticket holders.
2. Secure 12 preseason interviews with the stars of the team to create a marketing buzz.

Taking this example one step further, the Head Coach could extend this system by helping to set OKRs for both the Offensive Coordinator and the Defensive Coordinator. For the Offensive Coordinator, the Objective is to build the most dominant run attack in the league. To achieve it, the Key Results could be:

1. Make sure the offensive line is averaging seven pancake blocks per game.

2. Scheme four new run sets that the league has not seen from this team yet.

The Defensive Coordinator might have an Objective to build a top five defense in seven categories. To achieve this, Key Results could include:

1. Generating seven defensive line hurries per game.
2. 12 linebacker stops behind the line of scrimmage.

Transparency

One of the most effective components of an OKR system, whether it's for your advisory business or for an NFL franchise, is transparency. The Offensive Coordinator knows the OKRs of the General

Manager, the Head Coach, and the Head of Marketing. This transparency is what helps drive results because it keeps everybody on the same page and ensures accountability is perfectly clear.

Here is another example of how an OKR could work. Let's say my Objective is to *build adoption and establish thought leadership of the OKR framework in the financial advisor community.*

So, the Key Results I'm looking for each quarter to meet this Objective include:

1. Present the OKR system to 4,000 professional advisors.
2. Generate 2,000 OKR workbook downloads.
3. Start 100 quarterly OKR trials.

Through this framework, I can measure my Key Results every quarter. To the degree in which I am able to achieve them, I will know if my Objectives are being met.

Download an Excel or PDF Workbook that you can use as a financial advisor to build OKRs for yourself and your team by visiting jaycoulter.com/rab-okr.

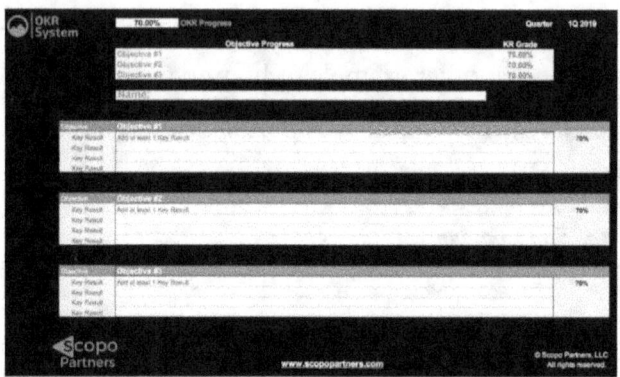

Sample OKR Worksheet

An OKR example for a financial advisory team:

Objective: Streamline our investment story and wealth management process.

Key Results:

1. Build a "Flagship" story with pitchbook.

2. Remove 25% of the orphaned funds in the book.

3. Convert 10 households to the new system.

For an analyst on the same team, the OKRs might be different:

Objective: Build consistency in the client investment matrix.

Key Results:

1. Identify 30 households for potential conversion and schedule the meetings.

2. Build actionable database of all orphaned funds.

3. Attend three training sessions on the "flagship story."

These examples should give you some ideas about how you can build OKRs for you and your team.

Simplicity and Measurement

One of the most important things to remember when you build OKRs is to make sure you keep them simple. Over-engineering OKRs tends to hurt results. You'll notice, in the downloadable Workbook, that there is a scorecard at the top. On this scorecard, you'll want to put in the quarter, because you'll want to keep track of your OKRs and results over time. You'll also notice a column with a percentage grading system for your OKRs.

Let's return to the Intel story. Operation Crush was a success. Andy and his team were able to remove Motorola as a competitive threat by leveraging nine simple OKRs. Those nine OKRs were then passed down through the entire organization. Line managers, sales managers and sales reps built their own OKRs to meet the Objective of crushing Motorola.

Andy Grove, the creator of OKRs, summed it up best when he describes OKRs as:

"...a very, very simple system."

But they do drive results. In fact, during the time period of Operation Crush, one of Andy's lieutenants came up with an even simpler formula for articulating OKRs—because nearly 1,000 employees were involved in the operation.

This manager simplified the process of building an OKR even farther. He narrowed it down to this simple formula:

Simple OKR Formula

I will __Objective__ as measured by __Key Result__.

The key word in the sentence above? *Measured.* An OKR system helps you measure your own results and measure the results of your team members in a very transparent way.

The 4 Key Benefits of OKRs

Here are the main benefits of using OKRs as a financial advisor:

1. They will help you focus and commit to priorities so you can keep your eye on the ball, and your teammates can keep their eyes on the ball.

2. They align teamwork, which gets rid of ambiguity surrounding what you're trying to achieve as a team or as a firm.

3. OKRs provide a clear mechanism for tracking accountability.

4. They help you build bigger and bigger goals.

OKRs and Leadership

As I'm sure you can see, there are multiple benefits to using an OKR system. What I have found while implementing this process into advisory practices is that it provides an excellent opportunity to demonstrate leadership and empower the various stakeholders in your organization.

1. Everyone on your team or in your firm can see exactly what you are focused on for the OKR period.

2. Everyone on your team can see how you as a leader are focused on your OKRs and the results you achieve.

3. As a leader, you are able to drive the high-level OKRs so your team can align with your vision.

4. Using this system, your team is empowered to make their own Key Results. This action drives ownership of the results.

Scheduled **OKR** Review Sessions

Experts on the OKR process say it is imperative that OKRs not be used as compensation evaluation tools. The OKRs should be very ambitious by design. As a leader, you do not want your team "sandbagging" their Key Results. In fact, you want your team to fall short of achieving 100% of their Key Results because they have set their goals incredibly high. In general, managers at Google and other companies hope to achieve about 70% of each Key Result. This system will not help you achieve dramatic growth if you are always achieving 100%!

Scheduled OKR Setting Sessions

Again, the OKR setting process provides an opportunity to both empower your team and demonstrate leadership. Let your team take the first stab at determining what their OKRs should be for the upcoming period, whether it is a month or a quarter. Then, have an open dialogue over the course of one or two meetings to solidify and mutually agree upon their OKRs.

Remember, the key to success is simplicity. Over-engineered OKRs will not get results!

Chapter 2: Building A Client Experience System

I have spent most of my career on the investment management side of the business. When I started consulting directly with financial advisors, teams, and firms, one thing stood out to me more than anything else. Most advisors are not confident they are taking good care of their clients. Shockingly, I have found a great majority of advisors feel an annual review, birthday card and some type of frivolous gift at Christmas counts as client service.

This lack of depth and low level of service is exactly why so many advisors struggle with the overwhelming feeling they just aren't doing enough for their clients. The unfortunate reality is they are not, and it is causing extreme stress.

Where to Start?

There are many great solutions and systems for financial advisors who are struggling with this aspect of their business. Naturally, I am biased towards my firms' **AB Client Touchpoint System** (scopopartners.com), but *any* reputable system will help your business.

I have had the opportunity to host Duncan MacPherson on my podcast, *The Resilient Advisor*. His firm, Pareto Systems, has a great client service system and philosophy on how to turn it into a referral system. Likewise, the folks at Supernova Consulting have had a positive impact on the businesses of many financial advisors I've encountered over the years. The team at The Oechsli Institute have a great program as well. I attended their *Rainmaker Weekend* a decade ago when I was working on an advisory team and their workshops are first class.

Why do I write so gushingly about my competition? Because I know, without exception, that if you implement any worthwhile client system, it will *change your life* as a financial advisor. I have witnessed careers take off thanks to the implementation of a thoughtful system. I have seen the dramatic impact on financial advisors and their entire teams. Building a high-functioning service system will not only give you more time in your day and increase the general happiness your people, it will create new business opportunities.

The Importance of a Touchpoint System

Before I explain how my system works, I would like to emphasize why a touchpoint system is so important. In my experience, most advisors struggle with bringing on new clients when they are not confident in their level of service to existing clients. It only makes sense: They are not able to enthusiastically solicit new relationships when they are not taking care of their existing ones! Fortunately, my system is radically simple by design. Complicated systems generally do not lead to success, and since using one is such an important part of your business as an advisor, it is imperative that it be simple and easy to use.

As I said, as a consultant, I have seen the implementation of a robust (but simple) client service system literally change careers. I am not being melodramatic here with my assertion. Once you build a system that you know has put you in the best situation to serve your clients, you will never again leave the office wondering if you have done all that you need to do to serve your clients. This reduces your stress and increases the time you have available in your day. That time can be given back to your family, used for charitable pursuits, or dedicated toward new business development.

If you are not sure whether you have a rock-solid client service system or not, answer this simple question:

What are your next three communication touchpoints with your fifth largest client?

Usually when I ask that question, I get the "deer in the headlights" look and the room falls silent. If this is you, please do not feel embarrassed as over 90% of the advisors I have worked with were not able to answer the question at the beginning of our consulting engagement.

The AB Client Touchpoint System

The backbone of your Client Experience System requires a well-thought-out and simple-to-execute process. The AB Client Touchpoint System empowers financial advisors.

There are five components of the AB Client Touchpoint System:

1. **Technology**

2. **Client Segmentation**

3. **Touchpoint Frequency & Type**

4. **Stress Testing Your System**

5. **Implementation**

Technology

Choose a technology provider that makes the most sense for your business. It could be your firm's CRM, Outlook, Redtail, Wealthbox or even an Excel-based program. The key to success with this system is simplicity as well as a recurring task function that runs in perpetuity.

If you are uncomfortable with CRMs or Excel, I would encourage you as an advisor to strongly consider reevaluating your attitude toward technology in your practice. The unfortunate reality is the advisor who relies on memory and luck will struggle to maintain their client relationships and grow their business.

Client Segmentation

Over the past two decades, I have seen many different types of segmentation programs. Generally speaking, they are always designed to benefit the person/company providing the analysis and segmentation. For example, the wirehouse analysis may have a bias toward encouraging lending, while an analysis built by an asset manager or insurance company usually supports allocations to their products. The ABZ Segmentation Process I recommend is designed to help you and your clients.

First, your client base should be segmented into three distinct groups (ABZ) outlined below. This starts with a quantitative analysis and is then modified using the advisor's subjective/qualitative lens. If you are not working with someone from my team, here is how you can build it yourself:

1. Create a list of your clients, prioritized by revenue, with the highest revenue client at the top.

2. Identify the top 50% of your revenue. Generally, advisors are surprised to find it's

only about 6-12% of the households in their book of business. This group of clients will start out as your "A" clients.

3. Identify the next 30% of your revenue and label them as "B" clients. Simple math reveals your "A" and "B" clients represent the top 80% of revenue in your book of business. By identifying how many clients drive 80% of your results, you are reverse engineering the Pareto Principle, which says 20% of your activity drives 80% of your results.

4. The bottom 20% should be labeled "Z" clients. I also called these clients "Anchors," as this group usually accounts for an outsized portion of the problems an advisor experiences in their business.

5. Next, apply the qualitative lens that only you, as the advisor, can use. Make sure your clients

are segmented in the most appropriate manner.

If you would like a complimentary **ABZ Client Segmentation & Analysis** run on your business that applies the quantitative lens in steps 1-4, please visit jaycoulter.com/rab-analysis.

Touchpoint Frequency & Type

Over the years, I have tried many different types of touchpoint systems. It is my strong opinion, based on real world application, that complicated systems do not work. The frequency and type of touchpoint added to a system is where the rubber meets the road, as they say. Success or failure comes down to simplicity.

Touchpoint Frequency: As outlined in the chart below, A clients will receive 12 touchpoints per year, of which four are "business" and eight are "social." The clients segmented B receive six touchpoints per year, with two of them in the "business" category and four in "social." It is radically simple by design.

Touchpoint Frequency

AB
Touchpoint
System

	Total Touchpoints	Business Touchpoint	Social Touchpoint
A	12	4	8
B	6	2	4

What you choose to do with clients in the Z segment is up to you. As a matter of best practice, I recommend at least one touch per year. Make sure to check with your firm's compliance officer to ensure you are doing the firm's required amount of touches at a minimum.

Touchpoint Type: In my opinion, this is where the complexity of most client experiences fails financial advisors. Systems that dictate daily activities on a granular level are difficult to execute over the long term. If the system is telling you to send an email one day to a client, then schedule a review a couple of weeks later, it will inevitably fail.

A robust system requires flexibility and that is what the AB Client Touchpoint System provides. Using this system, an advisor will have a choice, when prompted, to touch the client with either a business or social touch. The most popular types of touches for each of the categories are outlined in the graphic. The flexibility provided by the system to empower the advisor to choose the type of touch is what makes it so effective.

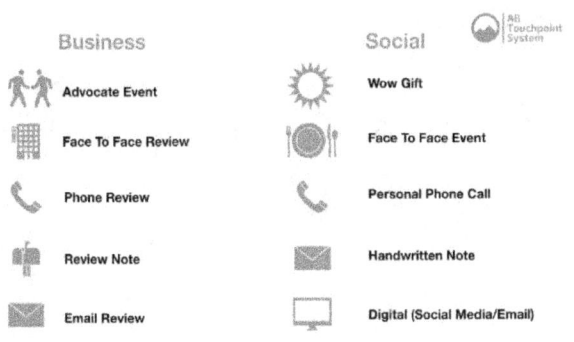

Business		Social	
	Advocate Event		Wow Gift
	Face To Face Review		Face To Face Event
	Phone Review		Personal Phone Call
	Review Note		Handwritten Note
	Email Review		Digital (Social Media/Email)

The Stress Test

A very important component of the system is the ability to understand *exactly* how much time you will be spending on proactive client service each year. Usually two things are very eye-opening to financial advisors when they examine the time commitment for their system. First, they don't need to spend as much time servicing their Z clients as they have been over the years. Second, they now have more free time in their business day to purse new clients. They are able to do this with confidence, knowing their existing clients are being taken care of systematically.

If you are using a reputable service provider, the system should be able to provide an estimate of the time you will spend on your outbound service touches.

Implementation

Now that you know exactly who you service, how often, and through which touchpoints, it is time to build your system in your chosen technology. If you're interested in learning how we help advisors implement their system using Excel-based software, please visit http://www.jaycoulter.com/rab-abresources

A Final Note on Your Client Experience System

Building and implementing a Client Experience System is a large undertaking. Over the years, I have found busy financial advisors are better served by hiring a consultant to help their team with the process than by trying to do it themselves. While this statement is indeed self-serving, it's also the truth. Results are seen faster and headaches are fewer. If you are serious about improving your client experience and growing your business, you will find it worth the investment.

Acres of Diamonds

There is an old story of an African farmer, as told often by Earl Nightingale, that has had an impact on the professional lives of thousands of people. Here is a condensed version:

A farmer heard tales about other people in his region who had made millions by discovering diamond mines. These tales so excited the farmer that he could hardly wait to sell his farm and go prospecting for diamonds himself. He sold his farm and spent the rest of his life wandering the continent searching unsuccessfully for the gleaming gems that brought such high prices. Worn out and in despair, he eventually threw himself into a river and drowned.

Meanwhile, the man who had bought his farm happened to be crossing the small stream on the property one day, when suddenly there was a bright flash from the stream bottom. He bent down and picked up a shiny stone, then brought it home and put it on his fireplace mantel as an interesting curiosity.

Several weeks later, a visitor picked up the stone, looked closely at it, and nearly fainted. He asked the farmer if he knew what he'd found. When the farmer said no, that he thought it was a piece of crystal, the visitor told him he had found one of the largest diamonds ever discovered.

The farm the first farmer had sold so that he might find a diamond turned out to be one of the most productive mines on the entire continent. **The first farmer had owned acres of diamonds. But he sold them for practically nothing in order to look for them elsewhere.** *If the first farmer had only taken the time to study and prepare himself to learn what diamonds looked like in their rough state, and to thoroughly explore the property he had before looking elsewhere, all of his wildest dreams would have come true.*

In my experience, every financial advisor has their own "Acres of Diamonds" in their personal and professional network. The *Revenue Model Matrix*

Exercise on the following page will help you mine your own farm to find those proverbial diamonds.

The Revenue Model Matrix Exercise

Step 1: Download the Revenue Model Matrix Excel worksheet: jaycoulter.com/rab-revenuemodeling

Step 2: Add your clients to the worksheet and segment using the following criteria:

Advocate: A client who has either referred or introduced you to a new high net-worth relationship in the past 18 months. These are the highest value clients.

Client: A relationship where you are handling all of their finances.

Customer: A relationship where you are handling only some of their finances. This clearly represents an opportunity to expand wallet-share.

Add-on: A relationship where you are handling their accounts because of a relationship they have with one of your other more profitable clients.

Step 3: Systematically review the worksheet and identify opportunities to turn customers into clients and clients into advocates as you work through your AB Client Touchpoint System.

Revenue Model Matrix

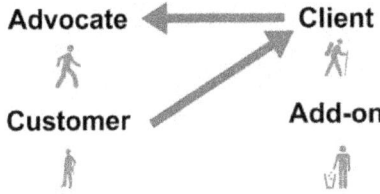

Chapter 3: Wealth Management System

Any financial advisor who has been in this business for a while has had a tough run professionally. The LTCM crisis was followed by the crash of the internet bubble in 2000. Once clients finally recovered, we were knocked right back down in 2008 with the financial crisis and the Great Recession. A friend of mine during that period, who had been in the business since the late 1990s, called me and asked, "What do I tell my clients who have been with me for 10 years and their accounts are lower today than when we started?" It was a fair question.

Despite all the challenges, however, this is a fantastic industry. Being a financial advisor is the best job in our economy. You have the opportunity for unlimited income and unlimited flexibility with your time, as well as the opportunity to have an impact on the lives of your clients. The price that comes with that opportunity is usually paid during periods of market turmoil. The way to ensure the best possible client outcomes during these periods is implementing a robust Wealth Management System.

Why Did You Get into This Business?

In the late 1980s, I was in high school and the movie *Wall Street* with Charlie Sheen and Michael Douglas was a box office hit. If you are not familiar with the plot, Bud Fox (played by the young Sheen) is an up-and-coming stock broker who seeks and finds mentorship from the unscrupulous corporate raider Gordon Gekko. I am sure director Oliver Stone's objective was to portray the evils of Wall Street, but my younger self was hooked on the idea of getting rich as a stock broker. I got into this business in the mid-90s because I loved investments.

Why did you get in this business? When I ask clients this question today, nobody says they got in this industry to do financial plans. Not one advisor has told me their passion is walking through a dry probate exercise with a retiring couple. Almost everyone came into this industry because of a passion or excitement around investments. I want to be clear, I am not encouraging you to become a portfolio manager if you are not comfortable managing money. But, it's time to put the "investment back" into *investment advisor*. To do so, it's crucial to know your investment story and where you compete as an advisor in your market.

Where Do You Compete?

When I was in graduate school at Emory University in Atlanta, one of the simplest models they taught has had the most lasting impact on how I look at business. It is a model designed to help companies identify where they compete. In simple terms, a company must be competitive in three different areas: Price, Product and Operational Excellence/Service. However, they can only COMPETE in one of those areas.

For example, when I give presentations to organizations and ask which Fortune 500 company competes on price, most of the time the response I get is Walmart. When I ask the same audience which company competes on product, Apple is usually the response. When I ask who competes on service, nine times out of 10, the Ritz-Carlton hotels are at the tip of everyone's tongue. Then I ask this question: Where do *you* compete as a financial advisor? One hundred percent of the time, the response is service. If everyone in your industry is competing in the same area, nobody is competitive in that area!

I believe today's financial advisor can differentiate themselves from the competition by competing on product. Note: I did *not* say performance. There is an important distinction and it comes down to branding. Let me explain.

Branding Your Portfolio

I'm very fortunate in my role as a coach and consultant in that I get to model what the top advisors in the country do to distinguish themselves. One area that very few advisors are able to show differentiation is in their investment offering. For the last two decades, financial advisors have been taught to allocate to firm-driven models, use mutual funds and other unnecessary packaged products, and get away from the business of being a financial advisor. If you want to differentiate yourself in your marketplace, develop an investment philosophy, story, and portfolio that enables you to stand out from the competition.

If you are not comfortable managing money, use one of your firm's models (or Outsourced CIO) and brand it as your own. In your conversations with clients, refer to *your* portfolio and process. I have learned the past several years, from advisors who take this approach, that clients love the fact that their financial advisor is managing their money. As a best practice, today's independent financial advisors are naming their portfolios after their firms. For example, *The Main Street Capital Core Portfolio* or *The Johnson Group Growth Strategy.*

When prospecting for new business, which do you think is more exciting to the prospect: another conversation with a guy who wants to talk about "Comprehensive Wealth Management," or a conversation with a knowledgeable financial advisor who is actually talking about an investment? This helps you put the "investment" back into investment advisor.

Branding Your Plan

Do you know the difference between the financial planning output from a wirehouse, an independent broker-dealer, or an RIA? The answer is *nothing!* Goldman Sachs is putting out the same financial plan as Charles Schwab. When you say the term "Financial Plan," it is wholly indistinguishable from the competition.

Today, we are seeing a trend where financial advisors, teams and firms are branding their financial plan. They use terms such as *process, method, system,* and *strategy* to distinguish their offering from the competition. For example, *The CCC Financial Planning System* or the *G4 Retirement Method* are used to help establish an engagement process and build brand awareness with their clients.

I have a turn-key system I allow clients to use called *The D6 Process - The Six Dimensions of Wealth.* When the markets turn, they are able to point to their branded process as opposed to specific returns in a particular account. If you've worked with clients during a market downturn, you know how impactful this can be to your conversations and your clients' decisions during periods of stress.

Referrals

Most industry research points to the clear fact that most new clients are acquired through referrals and introductions. Once you have a clearly branded investment and planning process, the referral process becomes exponentially easier. With a branded plan, your client knows what you do and how you do it. Now, they are able to better articulate it to potential referrals.

You will learn, in the following chapter on Relationship Marketing, that brand and influence are the core drivers of business growth today. The establishment of a brand centered on your process greatly enhances your success in the client acquisition game.

Chapter 4: Building A Relationship Marketing System

For the past several years, I have been teaching my *Connect and Influence* workshop via live events and webinars. These events are designed to be simple yet comprehensive, and, most importantly, actionable from day one. In these workshops, I teach participants how to build and engage with their networks, grow their professional influence and generate leads.

In the late nineties, I read a book on networking called *Never Eat Alone* by Keith Ferrazzi. To this day, it is still the best book I have read on business networking. In it, the author outlines the system he used to build his professional network and catapult his career. As someone who loves systems, I fell in love with it instantly. Over the years, I developed my own style and systems for staying connected with my network. These practices have evolved over time and I still continue to refine them today.

The core system I teach is called **The Pinger System**. It is the same system and strategy that I used to build my nonprofit into a brand with a global reach and over 200,000 followers on social media, and my personal reach to over 50,000 professionals. It enabled me to connect with volunteers and advocates all over the world. I have sold my books on five different continents and my podcast has been downloaded in over 100 countries. I would not have been able to accomplish any of this without the system I'll discuss here.

Social Selling is a Myth

In general, financial advisors are very skeptical professionals. This is quite understandable, given the nature of the profession and the wild roller coaster ride our careers have been the past several decades! Our skepticism, however, makes it incredibly difficult to move the needle when it comes to advisor participation and engagement with social media. I am reluctant to mention social media active monthly user statistics in a hard copy book because they change so rapidly. But, in general terms as of 2018, here are the numbers:

- Facebook: 2+ Billion
- Instagram: 1+ Billion
- LinkedIn: 550+ Million
- Twitter: 330+ Million

Consider this staggering fact: 76% of all Americans have a Facebook account. That means you can assume 76% of your clients and prospects are on the platform. What do they see when they come across your profile? How about LinkedIn? Instagram? These are massive platforms that provide access and opportunity for financial advisors who want to connect with more people and establish themselves as a thought leader in their market.

In my experience, this is where the problem for most advisors starts. There is a great opportunity here, yet most do not understand the application. This disconnect has facilitated the creation of nonsensical marketing scams and companies that promise untold riches if you just leverage their social media marketing program. Their marketing is slick and their promises are large, but I have yet to find one marketing program that delivers real results that are worth the price for financial advisors. Social selling is a myth, do not be fooled!

You are in the relationship business, not the mass marketing business. The opportunity with social media (and, in fact, in all digital media) lies in building your brand and influence using these platforms. This is a process that takes a long period of time and real work to make authentic connections. *This is a once-in-a-career opportunity to establish yourself as a thought leader in your market, but it is work and takes time.*

Why Most Advisors Don't Use Digital Media: The Common Objections

Seasoned professionals in any industry are always slow to adopt new technologies and opportunities. I remember, as a young stockbroker in the mid-1990s, there were a significant number of older advisors who refused to use email! Let's not even get started on having a website at the turn of the century. Eventually, these professionals had to adapt to the technology despite their reservations. Today, most financial advisors who are not active on social media give me one of these six excuses:

1. *"Compliance is too restrictive."*
2. *"My type of prospect does not use social media."*
3. *"I don't have the time."*
4. *"Big corporations like Proctor & Gamble are pulling out of social media marketing. Why would I waste my time?"*
5. *"I don't know what to say."*
6. *"I'll just pay someone to do it for me."*

On the surface, these excuses serve as enough reason for a financial advisor to not try to leverage social media in their marketing efforts. Let's face it, it sounds like work! However, this kind of short-term thinking will leave an advisor well behind his or her competition over time. Successful financial advisors utilize every method possible to be "known, liked and trusted."

For argument's sake, let me address these objections:

1. "Compliance is too restrictive."

There are no known compliance rules prohibiting you from having a personal Facebook account. If you choose not to have an active presence on the platform, it is your choice, not your firm's decision. Now, to be clear, just like in the non-digital world, a financial advisor needs to be judicious with their comments and presence on the platform. I recognize that a significant number of compliance departments limit functionality on LinkedIn, but that has loosened up significantly lately. As you will learn from my system, it is not what you post but who you connect with on a regular basis that drives results.

2. **"My type of prospect does not use social media."**

This statement is just an easy excuse as you know the statics on social media adoption. I hope you now know this is just not true. There will be valuable prospects that do not have an account on one particular social media platform or another. Yet this does not mean all of your prospects do not use those sites.

One of my favorite consulting exercises is when a client tells me that their clients are not on Facebook, I ask them to walk though their top 10 clients and we look to see if we can find these individuals on the site. Usually more than half have an active profile. Don't fool yourself, they are there!

3. "I don't have the time."

Before anybody starts building a digital marketing system, a simple question must be answered. Are you interested in investing the time to grow your business? If the answer is no, then please don't waste your time learning these different systems. It will just lead to frustration. But if you are serious about growing your business and live in the digital world we all find ourselves in today, you must make the time to build a digital footprint. This is a necessity if you want to remain relevant in our industry.

4. "Big corporations like Proctor & Gamble are pulling out of social media marketing. Why would I waste my time?"

People do business with people, not corporations. Who would want to follow P&G and see all of their advertisements about toothpaste and bleach? You are in the "people to people" business. People want to see what's going on in other people's lives. That is why reality television was and is so popular. It can be almost addictive to some folks. In fact, your rule of thumb regarding a particular marketing channel should be: The more corporations advertising in a particular space, the faster you should run the other way!

5. "I don't know what to say."

I understand this sentiment can be a difficult thing to get past at first, especially if you were raised to be humble. If you think people do not care about what you had for breakfast, you are correct. They do, however, care about what is actually going on in your life. The best guidance I have heard on this topic is to "document what you are doing." Try not to brag; nobody cares about your flamboyant vacation. However, they *do* care and would be interested in learning about a charity you care about. They do care about what's going on with your family.

During countless consulting meetings, I've had high functioning financial advisors tell me they would have nothing to say on social media while they spend most of our time together talking about everything that is going on in their lives. Everybody has something to say.

6. "I'll just pay someone to do it for me."

I cannot tell you how many times I've heard this one: A financial advisor outsources their social media to an intern or a third-party agency. As the late Jim Rohn used to say, "You can't pay someone to do your push-ups for you!" Connecting with people cannot be outsourced. There are components to your digital footprint that can be automated and outsourced, but those systems will never, ever result in you building a relationship.

The KLT Principle

The KLT Principle has been around since the beginning of the sales profession. People do business with people they "know, like and trust." Consider this concept throughout history. The door-to-door salesman who canvassed his community selling household goods at the beginning of the last century would have starved if not for building a reputation as someone who was known, liked and trusted. With the invention of print marketing and catalog sales in the 1920s and 30s, the door-to-door salesman became obsolete as print marketers built brands that were known, liked, and trusted.

Then came radio. The radio advertisements could reach you anywhere there was a transistor. The message was never stale, and the repeatable nature of marketing message made the brands using radio known, liked and trusted. Next, television slowly made its way into the forefront of sales and marketing. Slowly, over the course of decades, television brought you brands that became household names due to the fact that they were known, liked and trusted. TV marketing was the main benefactor of the KLT principle until the internet and email marketing started taking over. Its run as the predominant mechanism to achieving KLT status was short lived. Before anybody knew it, social media took over. If you doubt the power of social media and digital marketing, ask yourself these questions:

- *When was the last time you watched a television ad?*

- *When was the last time you looked at a billboard on the side of the road? (Chances are you had your face buried in your phone if you were not driving).*

- *When was the last time you clicked on a banner ad?*

- *When was the last time you opened junk mail that came out of your mailbox?*

- *When was the last time your SPAM filter did not catch an advertisement?*

The game of attention has changed. Forever.

Attention is on social media today. There, you will find birth and engagement announcements, along with other major life milestones of your clients and prospects. You can learn so much about your clients and prospects on social media that you're putting yourself at a disadvantage to your competition if you are not paying attention. And please trust me, your competition is there actively building their digital brand. If you want to be "known, liked and trusted," social media is where you will find the attention of your clients and prospects.

But it takes a system.

The Science of Influence

In his book *Influence: The Psychology of Persuasion,* Dr. Robert Cialdini provided the results of his research conducted over multiple decades on the topic of influence. Influence is just another term for sales and marketing. To this day, I believe this is one of the best books written on the topic.

Dr. Cialdini presents six "triggers" which drive influence. His research was conducted before the creation of social media, but four of the triggers have direct application to professionals who are trying to grow their professional network and influence.

These are detailed below:

> **Reciprocation:** In basic terms, this is the law of give and take. We are hardwired as humans to feel the need to return a favor. When someone shares, likes or comments on one of

your posts, it's human nature to feel the need to return the favor.

Liking: As simple as this trigger may seem, it cannot be discounted. We are drawn to and want to spend time with people we like. Our engagement and receptiveness to marketing messages goes up when we are communicating with someone we like. Social media is a great platform to help enhance this trigger.

Social Proof: Unfortunately, we are hardwired to be influenced by the opinions of others. That is why terms such as "bestselling" and "number 1 rated" are so common in marketing copy. This same concept has applications that result in triggers for professionals who are actively growing their network and influence on social media.

Authority: Humans are genetically disposed to trust people in positions of authority, unless that authority is abused. As you learn in my training program, it is simple to incubate an authoritative tone on social media that can have a long-term impact on your digital brand.

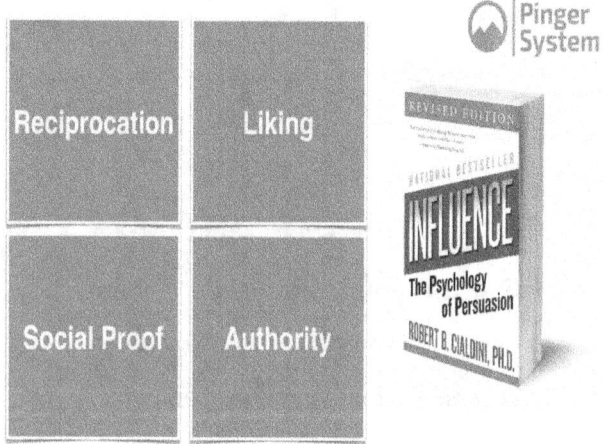

"Losers have goals…winners have systems."

~Scott Adams

The Pinger System

Building your professional network, brand, and influence in the digital age does not happen by accident. It takes a plan, a system, and *time*. If you are looking for a quick and easy solution to building your digital footprint, it is not going to be found here or anywhere else. If it was easy, everyone would do it and there would not be any value in it. What I am about to teach you is simple by design. But it is not easy. And you will never get results by paying someone to do this for you.

There are three modules to the *Connect & Influence* program. First, I'm going to teach you how to build a custom Pinger System that will enable you to stay connected with your network and manage your key relationships. Next, I will show you how to jumpstart your Pinger System with the Digital Supernova exercise. Last, I will show you how to build influence and cultivate leads by leveraging the BEEP Method.

It is very important that you do not skip ahead to the section on lead generation. If you do not have a Pinger System built to capture and manage your new connections and potential leads, you will just be wasting your time.

Building Your Pinger System

Your Pinger System is the backbone of your person to person (P2P) relationship marketing. It is designed to help you prevent those important, hard-fought connections from falling through the cracks. I am sure this scenario sounds familiar to you: You are at a social or business event and connect with someone who could be a good prospect or COI now or in the future. You swap cards and connect on LinkedIn. Then what happens? Nothing, typically!

The Pinger System helps solves that problem. Conceptually, it lets you know when it is time to "ping" someone you deem important to your networking or business efforts. It is designed to keep you "top of mind" in your network.

The 5 Components of a Pinger System

Building your system requires careful thought and consideration on the front end and will pay huge dividends once implemented. The devil is in the details.

There are five components to building your system:

1. Who
2. What
3. How
4. When
5. Where

1. **Who: Deciding who your most valuable connections are…and will be in the future!**

When deciding who should be added to your Pinger System, I recommend a simple two-step binary approach.

Step one: Is this person someone I want to stay connected with because of the value they bring to my networking efforts? Obviously, this is a yes or no question.

Step two: If I'm going to add them to my system, do I want to stay in touch with this individual on a regular basis because they are of high value, or would I prefer to just have an infrequent scheduled connection?

Let's apply some academic research to this part of the process. A study conducted by Professor Robin Dunbar at the University of Oxford, England found that most humans can only maintain friendships with about 150 people. Apparently, this is due to the size of a human brain. If we are at 150 capacity and add another friend, we actually lose connection with someone from our network. This makes it incredibly important to pay attention to who you put in your Pinger System. I will expand on this concept later.

2. **What: Defining a "Ping."**

A ping is a very simple, unscripted connection with someone. In his book *Never Eat Alone*, Keith Ferrazzi defined a ping as "a quick, casual greeting, and it can be done in any number of creative ways. Once you develop your own style, you'll find it easier to stay in touch with more people than you ever dreamed of in less time than you ever imagined." (Ferrazzi 2005)

It's difficult for me to expand on the definition from Keith, but I will point out that the key is to "develop your own style." When you have your own style, you will come across as both authentic and genuine in your communications.

It can be challenging to figure out what to say when it comes time to ping someone in your system. Here is my simple formula for generating ideas to add value to your contacts:

Who - Who in my network can I connect this person to for a mutually beneficial relationship?

What - What mutual connection points do we enjoy on personal or professional level?

How - How can I promote their causes or interests in my network?

3. **How: Which communications medium should I use for the ping?**

When I started in the investment business, my options for pinging were limited to a phone call, hand written note, and showing up at their house or place of business. Then, with technological advances, we could start leveraging email and texting to the extent our compliance department would allow it. Today, the game has changed again. Thanks to the powerful reach of social media, you are now able to like, comment, post and message your contacts on these platforms. This means there are well over nine different ways to ping your contacts in and unobtrusive manner. In addition, any posting that you do on these platforms just serves as "gravy" on top of your regular pings!

I have seen some systems in the marketplace that will tell you which type of ping to deliver when a name shows up in your list for the day. In my experience, this is a flawed system because you need the flexibility to use whichever ping is most appropriate at that point in time.

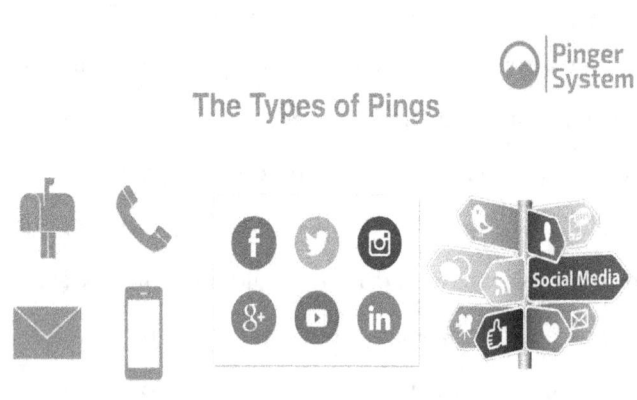

The Types of Pings

4. When: How often do you ping?

Next, you need to define your "ping cycles." By this, I simply mean: How often will you ping your contacts? I have built ping cycles of various sizes for myself and clients over the years. My first system had seven different cycles that included weekly, bi-weekly, monthly, bi-monthly, quarterly, bi-annual, annual and every two years. It was a massive system that had almost 1,500 contacts in it. After about a year, it failed miserably! This was before I had read Professor Dunbar's research.

Today, I use a very simple system for myself and my clients. If I add someone to my Pinger System, they are going to be contacted either **monthly, quarterly** or every **six months**. In my system, contacts are labeled **P1** (monthly), **P3** (quarterly) or **P6** (biannually) to denote the frequency of contact. After teaching financial advisors how to build these systems for the past three years, I can tell you the best results come from this simple cadence.

5. **Where: Selecting your technology**

It is imperative that you build a system on technology you are comfortable using on a daily basis. The greatest system in the world built on a complicated technology platform you are not comfortable using is *useless*. The main thing any system needs to have is a recurring task or reminder function that runs into perpetuity. Outlook, Salesforce, Act, Redtail, and Wealthbox will all work. I have built my own proprietary Excel-based system that you can download at jaycoulter.com/rab-pinger.

In addition to the recurring task or reminder function, there are three key components your technology platform must have:

1. Simplicity: If it is complicated, experience has taught me adoption goes down significantly after the first month.

2. Mobile Access: If you can 'ping' while in the airport or watching Little League, the utility of the system goes up exponentially.

3. Social Media Integration: If users can easily go from a contact screen to a LinkedIn or Facebook page, the pinging process is much easier.

Once you have built your Pinger System, it is time to jump start it with what I call the *Digital Supernova*.

Digital Supernova: Jump Starting Your Pinger System

Digital Supernova is a simple process I created to help my clients get some early wins in their relationship building efforts. The beauty of this system is that it does not cost anything except your time. It is also set up so your staff can help run this program for you.

I have had clients find great success with this program almost instantly after implementation. Most financial advisors uncover multiple six-figure opportunities. We have many stories of seven-figure relationships getting started and old friendships being reignited. One advisor shared with me a story in which he reconnected with a friend from high school he had not seen in decades. Two weeks later, this old friend and his wife were in that advisor's office putting together a retirement income plan.

Another advisor shared with me a situation in which he reconnected with a former client from 15 years earlier. When he reached out, the former client said, "I have been meaning to call you. I am about to retire and need some help." We later found out that he needed help because he had $15 million in stock options. **This system is not magic.** It simply creates a process for you to do the activities that you know you should have been doing all along.

Here is how it works:

1. Download your LinkedIn contacts into a CSV file. For instructions on exactly how to do this, visit the full tutorial and the download the **Digital Supernova Worksheet** at www.jaycoulter.com/rab-supernova

2. Copy and paste your LinkedIn contacts into the **Digital Supernova Worksheet**.

3. Go through each connection and label as such:

    1. **P1** - Someone you want ping once every month. (Don't designate more than 150 contacts this way.)

    2. **P3** - Someone you want to ping quarterly

    3. **P6** - Someone you want ping once every six months.

    4. **Client** - Someone who you don't need to ping because they are in your AB Client Touchpoint System. (See

chapter on your AB Client Touchpoint System for reference.)

5. **No** - Someone you don't need to ping at this time.

4. Add five 'P1' monthly pings per day to your Pinger System.

5. Add five 'P3" quarterly pings per day to your Pinger System.

6. Add two 'P6' bi-annual pings per day to your Pinger System.

Note: If you have the resources on your team, have your staff add the pings to your **Pinger System**.

After you have set up your Pinger System and completed the Digital Supernova exercise, you are ready for LinkedIn lead generation using *The BEEP Method.*

The BEEP Method - Building Influence & Lead Generation

The BEEP Method

BEEP is an acronym for **Build, Engage, Educate and Ping**. As you might imagine, it is a four-step process that requires customization to your unique brand and desired influence. This system is most effective when you have a niche in the market.

Here is the concept from a high level:

1. **Build:** Leveraging the optimal social media platform for your brand (most likely LinkedIn), script out a connection invitation that lays out the value proposition that speaks to WHY someone should connect with you.

   For example, my Connection Value Proposition as of this writing is: "I produce an industry podcast on practice management, the capital markets, and other issues advisors face called The Resilient Advisor. If you think it could add value to your business, here is a link: jaycoulter.com/listen. I would love to connect.

   While you most likely do not produce a podcast today, it is helpful to have a piece of valuable content to entice the initial connection.

2. **Engage:** The next step is to build out a sequence of touchpoints where each communication adds value to your new connection. Scripting out the engagement sequence is the most difficult part of this process. The reason this drives results is simply because so few people will put in the work to get this done.

This step in the process should be continually refined and changed as you are building your brand and influence. I use a software automation tool on LinkedIn as well as an email automation sequence leveraging MailChimp. If there's any part of this system to outsource, this would be it!

The end of your engagement sequence should have a call to action. That call to action could be a phone call, business meeting or a cup of coffee. Here is an example of an *Engagement Sequence*:

a. Connection Value Proposition and acceptance

b. Value-add Touch #1 (1 day later) - Deliver something of value!

c. Value-add Touch #2 (15 days after #1)

d. Value-add touch #3 (15 days after #2)

e. Value-add touch #4 (15 days after #3)

f. Value-add touch #5 (15 days after #3)

g. Call to Action Touch (Call, Meeting, etc.)

Notice you will have provided five *Value Touches* over a two-month period before you ever ask them for something in return (your call to action). In addition, you will be educating them about you and your brand during that incubation period with the next step in the BEEP Process: Educate.

3. **Educate:** This is the simplest part of the process, and thus yields the fewest results. I highly recommend creating your own original content through blogs, podcast or videos. If you are inclined, books and ebooks are incredibly effective. A robust education sequence simply involves posting on your preferred social media platforms on a regular basis.

   Note: if you outsource this to your firm or a marketing company that enables other advisors to post the same content, *you will not get results.* The algorithms on the social media platforms today will instantly pick up that multiple people are posting the same article and not deliver it to the feed of your network.

4. **Ping:** If someone has engaged with you through this process, but are not yet ready to become a client, it is imperative you *do not lose touch* with them. This is where your **Pinger System** comes into play. Apply these relationships to your system at the appropriate ping frequency to ensure you stay top-of-mind with these individuals. This helps guarantee you are the advisor of choice when they are ready to make a move!

The Impact List

For many financial advisors who have already reached a certain level of success, The BEEP Method is not necessary as it takes more of a shotgun approach to building their brand and influence. Experience has taught me that most seasoned advisors already know the families they would like to have as clients. I also know, however, that very few advisors put those families on a list or, more importantly, into a system to methodically nurture and build those relationships. This is where *The Impact List* will help you grow the relationships—on a granular level—that can have the highest impact on your business.

It is absurd the following statement is 100% accurate:

If you want to get a massive edge on your competition, make a list of your prospects.

I rarely run across an advisor who has a list of *any* prospects! **The Impact List** is designed to not only drive results by identifying your top prospects, but also by pushing you to build a list that will have a dramatic impact on your business over time. The Impact List process also methodically empowers you to find every possible connection point within your target so you can start building relationships and driving activity focused on the list.

Once you download the template for The Impact List, you or someone on your team needs to accumulate as much information as possible about the target. You will see that the information you need to acquire falls into three categories:

1. *Digital Profile*
2. *Work Profile*
3. *Personal Interests*

The objective is to identify as many potential connection points as possible while building a complete profile of your prospect. This is hard work. Very few advisors will take the time to do it, and that is why it works! As the old saying goes, "You have to do what others will not do in order to have what others will not."

As you build your Impact List, make sure to add them to your Pinger System so you are constantly building your influence and personal brand with them.

Download **The Impact List** template and watch the overview video here: jaycoulter.com/rab-impact.

The Influence 100

The legendary sales trainer Chet Holmes, in his book *The Ultimate Sales Machine*, outlined a process and system for identifying your "Dream 100" clients and then methodically building a sales process to acquire them. It is no longer 1997, and this does not work for financial advisors as a "sales" system. If it did, the advisors who made the highest number of cold calls would have the largest businesses, and everyone knows that is not how it works!

I have a different take on Chet's system that I have modified for today's financial advisor and today's interconnected world. **This tool is specifically for the financial advisor who wants to build their brand and influence inside of their niche and market**. As a disclaimer, this is very hard work. The goal of this system is to build credibility in your market by association **over a long period of time**. Find legitimate ways for them to see you, then you can set out to be seen with them in your market for credibility by association. This is a game of giving for an extended period of time before you will ever receive.

Download **The Influence 100** template for this process here: jaycoulter.com/rab-influence100.

Here is how it works:

1. Identify Influencers who serve your ideal clients, but don't compete with your services.

2. Break them into five groups:
    a. Bloggers
    b. Business Owners/List Owners
    c. Podcasters
    d. Social Media Influencer
    e. News Media (Print/Digital/TV)

3. Add your '*Influence 100*' to your Pinger System and methodically ping them once per month

or quarter to start building your brand awareness and shelf-space in their mind.

4. When the time is appropriate, reach out for a mutually beneficial collaboration.

A Final Thought on Relationship Marketing Systems

As you can see, the systems we've reviewed here are based on authenticity, a policy of providing real value, and relationship-building via regular contact. It's not easy to stay at the forefront of your prospects' minds, which is why it is so important to implement the systems in this section to ensure you and your team actual do it.

None of these systems are complex, but they are necessary if you want to grow your business as a financial advisor. Human beings are social creatures who make decisions based on relationships. Don't leave this piece of your business to chance!

Conclusion and Further Reading

Success as a financial advisor comes down to one thing: **systems**. In this book, I have described the exact systems I use in my coaching and consulting business to help advisors transition from practitioner to business owner.

I hope you've learned in these pages that building systems for the necessary tasks you must do to create a thriving financial advisory business can be freeing. I believe that you will also find them to be a requirement in order to keep up with the fast pace of change in our industry.

Implementing the systems we've discussed in these pages will give you peace of mind and help you grow your business. It is not possible to grow in any significant way without effective systems. Begin today, and don't hesitate to reach out to me for help.

Further 'Success Driver' Resources

Below is a list of the ten books that have had a dramatic impact on the systems I teach, the books I write and my personal life. To better understand *The Three Success Drivers* and apply them to your life, I highly recommend each of these works. These are books that every financial advisor should own and revisit on a regular basis.

Focus

- *Measure What Matters by John Doerr*
- *The One Thing* by Gary Keller & Jay Papsan
- *Start with Why* by Simon Sinek
- *The Magic of Thinking Big* by David Schwartz

Systems

- *Principles* by Ray Dalio
- *How to Fail at Anything and Still Win Big* by Scott Adams
- *The Compound Effect* by Darren Hardy

Relationships

- *Never Eat Alone* by Keith Ferrazi
- *Influence – The Psychology of Persuasion* by Dr. Robert Cialdini
- *How to Win Friends & Influence People* by Dale Carnegie

About Jay Coulter

Jay Coulter, CFP®, CIMA® is an investment strategist and practice management consultant. His businesses are focused on serving investors, financial advisors, teams and firms. Jay is also the host of The Resilient Advisor Podcast as well as the author of The Resilient Advisor (2017) and Conquer Worry (2016). Jay holds an M.B.A. from the Goizueta Business School at Emory University and a B.S. in Business Management from The University of Tennessee. Jay has earned the Certified Investment Management Analyst® and Certified Financial Planner® designations.

Connect with Jay:

Podcast: jaycoulter.com/listen

Twitter: twitter.com/sjaycoulter

Facebook: facebook.com/sjaycoulter

LinkedIn: linkedin.com/in/sjaycoulter

Instagram: instagram.com/sjaycoulter

YouTube: youtube.com/c/JayCoulter

The Resilient Advisory Business